Conserving America's Fisheries

U.S. Fish and Wildlife Service
Department of the Interior

Fisheries Program
Vision for the Future

December 2002

United States Department of the Interior

FISH AND WILDLIFE SERVICE

A Message from the Director

The U.S. Fish and Wildlife Service has a proud record of more than 130 years in fisheries and aquatic resource conservation. As Director, I am keenly aware of the need for a renewed commitment from the Service in conserving these valuable resources. Despite our proud heritage, we have become increasingly convinced of the need for greater support and resources if we are to be successful in meeting the challenges of our critical role in fisheries and aquatic resource management and conservation.

The Service is currently undertaking the task of describing the future role of its Fisheries Program in conserving this Nation's aquatic resources. I realize that the Service has undertaken planning exercises in the past. What is fundamentally different about this current effort is the development of a collaborative strategy with the Sportfishing and Boating Partnership Council and its Fisheries Steering Committee. This Steering Committee represents perspectives from a wide range of fisheries and aquatic conservation interests. This is an effective and powerful partnership that has worked well over a number of years, and I look forward to building on it as the Service strengthens and revitalizes its Fisheries Program.

The pride and passion of our Fisheries Program employees are clearly evident. They have carried us to where we are, in spite of difficult times. The Service has much to be proud of in our leadership in fisheries and aquatic resource conservation. Resolving real and perceived issues and revitalizing the Fisheries Program are among my highest priorities.

Steven A. Williams

Executive Summary

The Fisheries Program of the U.S. Fish and Wildlife Service (Service) has played a vital role in conserving and managing fish and other aquatic resources since 1871. Today, the Fisheries Program is a critical partner with States, Tribes, other governments, other Service programs, private organizations, public institutions, and interested citizens in a larger effort to conserve these important resources. The Nation's fish and other aquatic resources are among the richest and most diverse in the world. These resources have helped support the Nation's growth by providing enormous ecological, social and economic benefits. Despite efforts by the Service and others to conserve aquatic resources, a growing number are declining at alarming rates. Loss of habitat and invasive species are the two most significant threats to the diversity of aquatic systems. One-third of the Nation's freshwater fish species are threatened or endangered, 72 percent of freshwater mussels are imperiled, and the number of threatened and endangered species has tripled in the last 20 years. Clearly, there is increasing urgency to identify and implement actions that will reverse these alarming trends before it is too late.

In order to better conserve and manage fish and other aquatic resources in the face of increasing threats, the Service worked with partners to refocus its Fisheries Program and develop a vision. The vision of the Service and its Fisheries Program is working with partners to restore and maintain fish and other aquatic resources at self-sustaining levels and to support Federal mitigation programs for the benefit of the American public. To achieve this vision, the Fisheries Program will work with its partners to:

- *Protect* the health of aquatic habitats.
- *Restore* fish and other aquatic resources.
- Provide opportunities to *enjoy* the benefits of healthy aquatic resources.

In July, 2001, the Sport Fishing and Boating Partnership Council (SFBPC) was charged by the Service to convene a steering committee representing perspectives from a broad array of stakeholders in fish and aquatic resource conservation to work with the Fisheries Program during the development of a new blueprint for the future. This provided partners with a unique opportunity to be engaged before the strategic vision was drafted. It was also unique because the Fisheries Steering Committee included representatives from the Service, along with partners and stakeholders.

In January, 2002, the SFBPC Fisheries Steering Committee provided the Service with a set of consensus recommendations on the Fisheries Program's role in the partnership effort to conserve the Nation's fish and other aquatic resources. This report, entitled "A Partnership Agenda for Fisheries Conservation," along with the earlier SFBPC hatchery report, "Saving a System in Peril," were keystone elements in developing the Fisheries Program's strategic vision. Using these two reports and working collaboratively with partners, the Service has better defined its role in conserving and managing aquatic resources across the country. This strategic vision discusses where the Fisheries Program is today, where it needs to go in the future, and why it is important to get there. To move forward and be successful in this role, the Fisheries Program must be solidly supported, backed by sound science, and grounded in dynamic partnerships.

The Fisheries Program consists of almost 800 employees nationwide, located in 64 Fishery Resource Offices, including a Conservation Genetics Laboratory, 69 National Fish Hatcheries, 9 Fish Health Centers, 7 Fish Technology Centers and a Historic National Fish Hatchery. Together, these employees and facilities provide a network that is unique among Federal agencies, State and Tribal governments, and private organizations in its broad on-the-ground geographic coverage, its array of technical and managerial capabilities, and its ability to work across political boundaries and take a national perspective. It also brings to the aquatic conservation table the only Federal hatchery system, with extensive experience culturing more than one hundred different aquatic species.

The Fisheries Program and its partners recognize that they need to continue working together to identify actions that need to be initiated or expanded to achieve shared management goals, and then to address these needs or "gaps." The Fisheries Program and its partners also recognize that responsibilities for managing and conserving fish and other aquatic resources are shared, and success is usually contingent on partnerships that cut across jurisdictions and link all stakeholders and partners. Resource objectives and Federal, State and Tribal roles have also shifted over time. Where once the Service focused primarily on restoring and managing game species, its conservation mission has expanded, and today includes non-game and endangered species. Just as important, the Service and its partners know that the opportunities, challenges, and needs facing aquatic resources exceed budgetary resources, as well as Federal authorities and responsibilities. Consequently, the Fisheries Program will use five criteria in deciding what activities, opportunities, and issues to address for each of the seven priority areas set out in this strategic vision. Current and potential actions will be evaluated against the following criteria, and partners will be consulted as key decisions are made that affect the direction of the Fisheries Program. The Service will weigh potential actions by:

- The strength of Federal authority and responsibility;
- The extent to which our efforts will complement others in the fisheries and aquatic resource conservation community;
- The likelihood that our efforts will produce measurable resource results;
- The likelihood that our efforts will produce significant economic or social benefits; and
- The extent of partner support.

The Service will also ensure that actions taken by the Fisheries Program will be consistent with strategic plans being developed by the Department of the Interior and the Service as a whole, and that Fisheries Program actions will help achieve performance targets laid out in those plans. The Fisheries Program's strategic planning effort is proceeding parallel to the strategic planning efforts being conducted by the Department and the Service. These planning efforts have been closely coordinated to ensure agreement and consistency among the three levels of management.

The Service is re-committing to its role as a partner in conserving America's fish and other aquatic resources. In some cases, the Fisheries Program will lead; in others, it will facilitate or follow. In all cases, the Fisheries Program will focus its efforts and activities on what it is best positioned to contribute based on its unique resources and capabilities, recognizing that sound science and solid partnerships will continue to be the key to aquatic resource stewardship. Working with its partners, the Fisheries Program has identified seven areas of emphasis with associated goals, objectives, and actions to focus on in the future. In some cases, these actions reflect a reaffirmation of current activities; in other cases, they reflect some change in those activities. In a few cases, the actions reflect a new activity for the Fisheries Program. Many of its current activities support these goals and objectives, and there will be some opportunities to refocus and change within existing resources. However, the scope and speed with which this blueprint for the future becomes reality will depend on the level of support and resources that are available to the Fisheries Program. The seven focus areas that the Fisheries Program will take actions to emphasize are:

- Partnerships and Accountability;
- Aquatic Species Conservation and Management;
- Public Use;
- Cooperation with Native Americans;
- Leadership in Science and Technology;
- Aquatic Habitat Conservation and Management; and
- Workforce Management.

Introduction

Since 1871, the Fisheries Program of the U.S. Fish and Wildlife Service (Service) has played a vital role in conserving and managing this Nation's aquatic resources. Over the years, the Service has been a leader in almost every aspect of fisheries management, fish health and fish culture. Today, the Fisheries Program is a critical partner with other Service programs, States, Tribes, other governments, private organizations, public institutions, and interested citizens in a larger effort to conserve fish and other aquatic resources. The Service asked a broad array of these partners to help identify the most critical needs for aquatic resources and to reach consensus on the most appropriate role for the Fisheries Program. The new vision for the Fisheries Program was developed with their help.

Vision

The vision of the Service and its Fisheries Program is working with partners to restore and maintain fish and other aquatic resources at self-sustaining levels and to support Federal mitigation programs for the benefit of the American public.

Implementing this vision will help the Fisheries Program do more for aquatic resources and the people who value and depend on them through enhanced partnerships, scientific integrity, and a balanced approach to conservation.

Status of the Nation's Fish And Other Aquatic Resources

The Nation's fish and other aquatic resources are among the richest and most diverse in the world. These resources, and the recreational, commercial, and subsistence opportunities they provide, have helped support the Nation's growth by providing enormous ecological, social and economic benefits. Preliminary surveys conducted by the Service show that recreational fishing contributed more than $35 billion annually to the American economy in 2001 alone. An economic analysis conducted independently by the American Sportfishing Association in 1996 showed that recreational fishing's overall economic impact to the economy was $108.4 billion, including 1.2 million jobs and $28.3 billion in personal income (ASA 1996). Fish and aquatic resources are particularly important to our Nation's Native American communities which rely upon healthy, sustainable natural resources to meet subsistence, economic, ceremonial, religious, and medicinal needs.

Despite efforts by the Service and others to conserve fish and other aquatic resources, a growing number are declining at alarming rates. Almost 400 aquatic species either have, or need, special protection in some part of their natural or historic range (Williams et al. 1989; Moyle and Leidy 1992). The number of species listed as threatened or endangered under the *Endangered Species Act* in 2002 has increased to 19 amphibian species, 21 crustacean species, 70 mussel species, and

115 fish species. Several threatened and endangered species of fish are important recreational, subsistence, and commercially species, including several species or populations of salmon, sturgeon, and trout. Of the 297 species of freshwater mussels in the U.S., 213 (72 percent) are threatened, endangered, or of special concern (Williams et al. 1993). None of these aquatic species or populations have ever been removed from the *Endangered Species Act* list, although a few are close to being de-listed or down-listed from endangered to threatened.

The reasons for these declines are linked largely to habitat loss or alteration (including flow changes, watershed modifications, sedimentation and pollution) and the impacts of harmful exotic or transplanted species. Healthy stream and riparian habitats are critical to the sustainability of all aquatic resources. Approximately 53 percent of the Nation's 221 million acres of wetlands have disappeared (Dahl 1990). Today, 185 species of fish and 88 species of mollusks are found in the U.S. that have been introduced from every continent except Antarctica (Fuller et al. 1999; OTA 1993). While some of these species create significant economic benefits, others, such as zebra mussels, Asian clams, and Asian carps cause significant harm to native fish and other aquatic resources. Native fish and other aquatic resources are especially threatened by these invaders because of their rapid spread through connected waterways. Since the unintentional introduction of zebra mussels into the Great Lakes, the number of native mussel species in the east channel of the Mississippi River near Prairie du Chien, Wisconsin, decreased from more than 30 to only 7 species during a 4-year period (Miller and Payne 2001). Clearly, the Nation is at risk of losing its diverse aquatic resources and the critically important benefits they provide.

Biological and social scientists, government agencies, conservation groups, and the American public are becoming increasingly concerned about the decline of fish and other aquatic resources and the economic impact of those declines. They point with increasing urgency to actions that must be taken to reverse these alarming trends. Management and conservation actions for virtually all fish and other aquatic resources are a shared responsibility. Success in reversing the trend will rely on continuing partnerships and forging new partnerships that cut across jurisdictions and link stakeholders and partners.

Over time, resource objectives and Federal, State and Tribal roles have shifted. Where the Service once focused primarily on restoring and managing game species, the conservation mission has changed and today, includes non-game and endangered species. These new realities led the Service to re-examine its Fisheries Program's existing obligations and to explore the appropriate balance between State, Tribal and Federal responsibilities. Working collaboratively with its partners, the Service has better defined its role in conserving and managing aquatic resources across the country. To move forward, the Service and its Fisheries Program must be solidly supported, backed by sound science, and grounded in dynamic partnerships.

How This Effort Is Different

In July, 2001, the Sport Fishing and Boating Partnership Council (SFBPC) was charged by the Service to convene a steering committee representing perspectives from a broad array of stakeholders in fish and aquatic resource conservation to work with the Fisheries Program during the development of a new blueprint for the future. This provided partners with a unique opportunity to be engaged before the strategic vision was drafted. It was also unique because the Fisheries Steering Committee included representatives from the Service, along with partners and stakeholders.

In January, 2002, the SFBPC Fisheries Steering Committee provided the Service with a set of consensus recommendations on the Fisheries Program's role in the partnership effort to conserve the Nation's fish and other aquatic resources. This report, entitled "A Partnership Agenda for Fisheries Conservation," along with the earlier SFBPC hatchery report, "Saving a System in Peril," were keystone elements in developing the Fisheries Program's strategic vision. The Service also used GAO reports, ongoing interactions with the SFBPC Fisheries Steering Committee, Service employees, and the Service work group efforts to address the 24 hatchery-related directives from the Department of the Interior and the Office of Management and Budget to better defined its role in conserving and managing aquatic resources across the country.

The Service is re-committing to its role as a partner in conserving America's fish and other aquatic resources. In some cases the Service will lead; in others, it will facilitate or follow. In all cases, the Service will focus its efforts and activities on what it is best positioned to contribute based on its unique resources and capabilities, recognizing that sound science and solid partnerships will continue to be the key to aquatic resource stewardship. The Service will work closely with its partners on an ongoing basis to refine and adapt its Fisheries Program activities within this framework to effectively respond to priority needs and issues.

The Service's Fisheries Program

The Service's Fisheries Program consists of almost 800 employees nationwide, located in 64 Fishery Resources Offices, including a Conservation Genetics Laboratory, 69 National Fish Hatcheries, 9 Fish Health Centers, 7 Fish Technology Centers and a Historic National Fish Hatchery. Together, these employees and these facilities provide a network that is unique among Federal agencies, State and Tribal governments, and private organizations in its broad on-the-ground geographic coverage, its array of technical and managerial capabilities, and its ability to work across political boundaries and take a National perspective.

This network stands out, but it does not stand alone. Its main strength is its ability to work collaboratively with partners on almost any issue, problem or opportunity to conserve or restore the Nation's fish and other aquatic resources. Another strength is its ability to bring unique capabilities that individual States and Tribes often lack because of their narrower authorities and jurisdictions. For example, the Fisheries Program's National Fish Hatchery System, the only Federal fish hatchery system that exists, has extensive experience culturing more than one hundred aquatic species, including fish, mussels, plants, amphibians and invertebrates. By sharing capabilities at National Fish Hatcheries, Fish Technology Centers, and Fish Health Centers, Service fisheries biologists can lead or participate in cooperative programs related to fish health, nutrition, and water use technology. Similarly, field biologists in Fishery Resources Offices serve a vital role in restoring, managing, and conserving the health of nationally significant fish and other aquatic resources and the habitats they depend on. Biologists develop scientifically sound data and information to improve the health of populations and their habitats, diagnose problems, prescribe solutions, and coordinate diverse efforts. The broad geographic responsibilities of these biologists often enable them to reach across State and Tribal boundaries, as well as agency jurisdictions, to craft coalitions, partnerships and solutions.

Our Commitment

The vision of the Service and its Fisheries Program is working with partners to restore and maintain fish and other aquatic resources at self-sustaining levels and support Federal mitigation programs for the benefit of the American public. To achieve that dream, the Fisheries Program is committed to working with our partners to:

- *Protect* the health of aquatic habitats.
- *Restore* fish and other aquatic resources.
- Provide opportunities to *enjoy* the many benefits of healthy aquatic resources.

Making Decisions and Setting Priorities

The crisis facing the Nation's fish and aquatic resources demands the attention of Federal, State, and Tribal resource management agencies, conservation and environmental organizations, and the American public. The Fisheries Program embraces a balanced approach toward aquatic resource stewardship that recognizes the need to conserve and manage self-sustaining populations and their habitats, and at the same time, provide quality opportunities for responsible fishing and other related outdoor activities.

Opportunities, challenges, and needs facing aquatic resources exceed budgetary resources, as well as Federal authorities and responsibilities. With the help of partners, the Service and its Fisheries Program has identified seven priority areas where it can and should make a difference. These priority areas are listed below, and include goals, objectives, and actions which include reaffirming some current activities, refocusing others, and starting new ones. This strategic vision document is intended to focus and direct Fisheries Program activities over the next 10 years.

The Fisheries Program will use five criteria in deciding what fishery activities, opportunities, and issues to address for each of the seven priority areas, and partners will be consulted as key decisions are made that affect the direction of the Fisheries Program. The criteria are based on the identification of a Federal role and a determination of whether or not the Service is the most appropriate Federal agency. The Service will weigh proposed and potential activities by:

- The strength of Federal authority and responsibility;
- The extent to which our efforts will complement others in the fisheries and aquatic resource conservation community;
- The likelihood that our efforts will produce measurable resource results;
- The likelihood that our efforts will produce significant economic or social benefits; and
- The extent of partner support.

Implementation Actions

The implementation actions included in this strategic vision document focus on the key actions the Fisheries Program believes it needs to take to attain the vision. They also focus on actions that will make the Fisheries Program more effective in conserving aquatic resources, meeting the needs of American citizens and establishing partnerships. Each objective in this strategic vision is supported by one or more implementation actions. These actions were chosen and described to be specific, measurable, accountable, and results-oriented. Their order does not indicate an order of importance. The scope and speed with which these actions can be taken will depend on the support and resources available to the Fisheries Program.

Determining the Service's success in implementing this strategic vision will be based on monitoring and evaluating accomplishments. Equally important is communicating successes and failures to our partners, stakeholders, Congress, and the Administration. Meetings will be held each year to communicate progress and accomplishments. A report to Congress will be written biennially. This strategic vision with its implementation actions serves as a general contract between the Service and its partners. It identifies key actions the Service and its Fisheries Program will take in the interest of conserving America's fish and other aquatic resources and in sustaining the benefits those resources provide.

The implementation actions included in this report draw on a number of sources, most significantly the two SFBPC reports, ongoing interaction with the SFBPC Fisheries Steering Committee, Service employees, and the Service work group efforts to address the 24 hatchery-related directives from the Department of the Interior and the Office of Management and Budget. Some of the work group responses to the hatchery directives are still in development and will be added as appropriate when they are finalized. The implementation actions also draw on twelve issue papers that were exchanged between the Service and the Steering Committee during development of the two SFBPC reports, and that proved invaluable in identifying actions that should be undertaken or expanded to help fill in gaps in the collective capabilities of the Service and its partners.

Success in implementing this strategic vision for the Fisheries Program hinges on developing step-down actions that are specific to each of the seven geographic regions of the Service and its Fisheries Program headquarter's office. These 5 year step-down plans will identify specific activities that will contribute to the strategic vision and identify annual targets that link back to Departmental and Service strategic plans developed under the *Government Performance and Results Act* (GPRA). The regional Fisheries Program step-down plans will establish accountability for each activity by identifying responsible parties, due dates and end products or outcomes. Linkages among activities will also be identified, as will factors and prerequisites that might be especially important to successfully completing those activities. The plan for the Fisheries Program headquarters office will dovetail with the seven regional step-down plans and facilitate successful implementation of activities in those plans. Where two or more regions have common issues, they will coordinate the development of activities. All eight step-down plans will be assembled as a compendium, made available broadly on the Internet, and used in planning and operations to set direction and promote communication, understanding, accountability and partnerships. All eight plans and the Strategic Plan for the Fisheries Program will include components to ensure and promote financial accountability.

The Fisheries Program's strategic planning effort is proceeding parallel to the strategic planning efforts being conducted by the Department and the Service. These planning efforts have been closely coordinated to ensure agreement and consistency among the three levels of management. Tasks conducted under the Fisheries Program's Strategic Plan will support four goals under the Department's major goal areas:

> RESOURCE PROTECTION
> !   Goal #1: Watersheds, Landscapes, and Marine Resources
> !   Goal #2: Biological Communities
> RECREATION
> !   Goal #2: Ensure Quality Experience and Enjoyment of Natural and
>   Cultural Resources on DOI Managed and Partnered Lands and Waters
> SERVING COMMUNITIES
> !   Goal #3: Fulfill Indian Trust Responsibilities

Performance measures and performance targets will be developed as the strategic plan for each management level is stepped down into outcomes, actions, and tasks. Core performance measures will be the same under the strategic plans for all three levels of management. Furthermore, a small number of additional performance measures specific to the Service or to the Fisheries Program may be developed during the Regional step-down planning process. The Regional step-down plans will be rolled back up and assembled into the Strategic Plan for the Service's Fisheries Program. The common, core performance measures will link the Fisheries Strategic Plan to the Service's Strategic Plan, and then to the Department's Strategic Plan.

Goals, Objectives, and Actions

The Service will strengthen and revitalize its Fisheries Program and re-commit itself to partnership efforts to conserve the Nation's fish and other aquatic resources, focusing on seven priority areas: Partnerships and Accountability, Aquatic Species Conservation and Management, Public Use, Cooperation with Native Americans, Leadership in Science and Technology, Aquatic Habitat Conservation and Management, and Workforce Management. The order of these priority areas is not intended to imply a relative priority. Goals, objectives, and actions have been identified for each of the seven priority areas.

1. Partnerships and Accountability

Partnerships are essential for effective fisheries conservation. Many agencies, organizations, and private individuals are involved in fisheries conservation and management, but no one can do it alone. Together, these stakeholders combine efforts and expertise to tackle challenges facing fisheries conservation. The success of these partnerships will depend on strong, two-way communications and accountability. Goals, objectives, and actions were developed to direct Fisheries Program efforts for working with partners and being accountable.

Partnership Goal: Open, interactive communication between the Fisheries Program and its partners. The Fisheries Program will develop and improve relationships with partners, focusing on the following areas:

Objective 1.1: Develop and improve long-term partnerships with States, Tribes, other federal agencies, non-governmental organizations (NGOs), and other Service Programs to develop collaborative conservation strategies for aquatic resources.

> *Action 1.1.1:* Facilitate annual meetings in each Region with State Fish and Wildlife Agencies, Tribal representatives, NGOs, other federal agencies, and Service counterparts to identify and resolve aquatic resource management problems, explore new management opportunities, and maintain productive working relationships.

> *Action 1.1.2:* Explore new opportunities to improve government-to-government relationships with Tribal governments.

> *Action 1.1.3:* Establish new "Friends Groups" to support the goals and purposes of the associated hatchery or other Fisheries facility with annual objectives established on regional and national levels.

> *Action 1.1.4:* Work with other Service Programs to leverage available funding and expertise, and maximize the attainment of aquatic resource conservation goals.

Accountability Goal: **Effective measuring and reporting of the Fisheries Program's progress toward meeting short-term and long-term fish and other aquatic resource conservation goals and objectives.** The Fisheries Program will develop effective accountability measurements and reporting, focusing on the following areas:

Objective 1.2: Develop and implement performance measures to determine the efficiency and effectiveness of Fisheries Program resource activities and financial accountability.

> *Action 1.2.1:* Develop and implement regional and headquarters step-down plans, tiered from the Service's Fisheries Program strategic vision within 6 months after the finalization of this strategic vision.

> *Action 1.2.2:* Annually monitor and evaluate Regional and National progress toward meeting specified performance measures, including *Government Performance Results Act* (GPRA) performance measures, and report on its related accomplishments.

> *Action 1.2.3:* Develop performance measures to evaluate the effectiveness and efficiency of its activities relative to the strategic vision, starting in FY04, using both internal evaluations and input from States, Tribes, NGOs, and other federal agencies to measure progress toward meeting expectations.

> *Action 1.2.4:* Manage Fisheries Program funding to maximize Program performance and to allocate and spend Program funds in a timely and responsible manner.

2. Aquatic Species Conservation and Management[1]

The Fisheries Program maintains and implements a comprehensive set of tools and activities to conserve and manage self-sustaining populations of native fish and other aquatic resources. These tools and activities are linked to management and recovery plans that help achieve restoration and recovery goals, provide recreational benefits, and address Federal trust responsibilities. Sound science, effective partnerships, and careful planning and evaluation are integral to conservation and management efforts. Goals, objectives, and actions were developed to direct Fisheries Program efforts for Native Species, Aquatic Nuisance Species, and Interjurisdictional Fisheries.

Native Species

Habitat degradation and the spread of aquatic nuisance species are causing many native species populations to decline. One hundred fifteen species of fish, 19 species of amphibians, 70 species of mussels, and 21 species of crustaceans are listed as threatened or endangered under the *Endangered Species Act*. Many other unlisted species are also in decline.

---

[1] For activities related to introduced and naturalized species, please see the Public Use section.

Native Species Goal: **Self-sustaining populations of native fish and other aquatic resources that maintain species diversity, provide recreational opportunities for the American public, and meet the needs of tribal communities.** The Fisheries Program will conserve native fish and other aquatic resources, focusing on the following areas:

Objective 2.1: **Recover fish and other aquatic resource populations protected under the *Endangered Species Act*.** The Fisheries Program will increase efforts in planning and implementing actions with partners to help recover threatened and endangered aquatic species, such as developing rearing technologies and providing refugia, while restoring aquatic habitats.

> *Action 2.1.1:* Provide increased expertise to the Endangered Species Program to conduct status reviews for fish and other aquatic resources populations.

> *Action 2.1.2:* Identify threatened and endangered fish and other aquatic species that do not currently have recovery plans and update the list on an annual basis, in coordination with the Endangered Species Program.

> *Action 2.1.3:* Take the lead in working with Endangered Species Program staff and partners to develop recovery plans for those threatened and endangered species identified in Action 2.1.2.

> *Action 2.1.4:* Increase implementation of appropriate actions identified in recovery plans.

Objective 2.2: **Restore declining fish and other aquatic resource populations before they require listing under the *Endangered Species Act*.** The Fisheries Program will increase its support and assistance in stopping and reversing declines of native fish and other aquatic resources, including restoring fish passage and rebuilding populations.

> *Action 2.2.1:* Work with States, Tribes, the Endangered Species Program, and other key partners to identify declining fish and other aquatic resource populations and the associated threats.

> *Action 2.2.2:* Work with States, Tribes, and other partners to identify and prioritize actions that will be most effective and efficient in achieving desired resource goals and outcomes.

> *Action 2.2.3:* Work with States, Tribes, and other partners to begin implementing identified priority actions to eliminate or reduce the threats causing the declines.

Objective 2.3: **Maintain diverse, self-sustaining fish and other aquatic resource populations.** The Fisheries Program will increase its participation in collaborative efforts to ensure that habitats and native biological communities remain intact and at self-sustaining levels.

Action 2.3.1: Work with States, Tribes, and other federal agencies to monitor the status of self-sustaining native fish and other aquatic resource populations and to identify the biggest threats to those populations.

Action 2.3.2: Work with States, Tribes, and other federal agencies to identify and implement priority actions that need to be taken to reduce and monitor the biggest threats.

Aquatic Nuisance Species
Aquatic nuisance species threaten the diversity or abundance of native species or the ecological stability of infested waters, or commercial, agricultural, aquacultural or recreational activities dependent on those waters. More than 20 Federal agencies are involved with preventing and controlling aquatic nuisance species, in cooperation with States, Tribes, private industry, and others.

Aquatic Nuisance Species Goal: **Risks of aquatic nuisance species invasions are substantially reduced, and their economic, ecological, and human health impacts are minimized.** The Fisheries Program will seek to prevent and reduce the establishment and spread of aquatic nuisance species, focusing on the following areas:

Objective 2.4: **Prevent new introductions of aquatic nuisance species.** The Fisheries Program will increase its leadership role in collaborative efforts to implement activities and programs that prevent the establishment of aquatic nuisance species.

Action 2.4.1: Increase efforts to work with the Aquatic Nuisance Species Task Force, the National Invasive Species Council, and others to identify and monitor high-risk pathways for the introduction of Aquatic nuisance species and to participate in preventative actions to reduce the likelihood of the introduction of new aquatic nuisance species associated with those pathways.

Action 2.4.2: Facilitate the prevention and control of aquatic nuisance species through the development and support of State management plans, regional panels and other mechanisms.

Action 2.4.3: Coordinate the Service's efforts in the re-authorization of the National Invasive Species Act.

Action 2.4.4: Increase education and outreach activities to raise public awareness of aquatic nuisance species problems and how the public can help.

Action 2.4.5: Implement Hazard Analysis and Critical Control Points (HACCP) or similar control planning processes in the National Fish Hatchery System and other Fisheries Program activities to prevent the unintentional release or spread of aquatic nuisance species.

Objective 2.5: **Minimize range expansion and population growth of established aquatic nuisance species.** The Fisheries Program will expand its role in partnership efforts by developing methods and conducting programs designed to prevent the spread of aquatic nuisance species to new locations and limit growth of established populations.

> *Action 2.5.1:* Increase efforts to work with States, Tribes, and other partners by coordinating surveys and monitoring efforts to detect and control aquatic nuisance species.

> *Action 2.5.2:* Work with the National Wildlife Refuge System, States, Tribes, other federal agencies, and NGOs to increase rapid response and other capabilities to control aquatic nuisance species populations and prevent their expansion.

Interjurisdictional Fisheries
Responsibility for managing native, interjurisdictional fisheries in the United States is assigned by many laws, treaties, and court orders, but follows no single model. By definition, interjurisdictional fisheries management is a collaborative process involving State, Tribal and Federal governments.

Interjurisdictional Fisheries Goal: Interjurisdictional fish populations are managed at self-sustaining levels. The Fisheries Program will support, facilitate and/or lead collaborative approaches to conserve, and where necessary restore, sustainable interjurisdictional fish populations, focusing on the following areas:

Objective 2.7: **Co-manage interjurisdictional fisheries.** The Fisheries Program will increase its participation and assistance with other Federal, State, and Tribal interjurisdictional fishery management efforts, including commercial and subsistence fisheries in freshwater, coastal, and marine ecosystems.

> *Action 2.7.1:* Lead the development of a Memorandum of Understanding to clarify the roles and responsibilities of the Service and the National Marine Fisheries Service in managing interjurisdictional fisheries.

> *Action 2.7.2:* Increase participation in interstate fishery management councils, commissions, and other associations.

> *Action 2.7.2:* Provide Federal leadership to implement the Federal subsistence fisheries program in Alaska, pursuant to mandates of the Alaska National Interest Lands Conservation Act.

Objective 2.8: **Support, facilitate, and/or lead collaborative approaches to manage interjurisdictional fisheries.** The Fisheries Program will increase its involvement in collaborative efforts, including the development of fishery and watershed management plans, collect and share scientific information and data, and provide fish required under fishery management plans.

> *Action 2.8.1:* Work with States, Tribes, and other federal agencies to identify the biggest threats to maintaining self-sustaining, interjurisdictional fish populations in freshwater, coastal, Great Lakes and marine ecosystems.

> *Action 2.8.2:* Work with States, Tribes, and other federal agencies to identify and implement priority actions to eliminate or reduce those threats.

3. Public Use

As the population in the United States continues to grow, the potential for adverse impacts on aquatic resources, including habitat will increase. At the same time, demands for responsible, quality recreational fishing experiences will also increase. The Service has a long tradition of providing opportunities for public enjoyment of aquatic resources through recreational fishing, habitat restoration, and education programs and through mitigating impacts of Federal water projects.

The Service also recognizes that some aquatic habitats have been irreversibly altered by human activity (i.e. - dam building). To compensate for these significant changes in habitat and lost fishing opportunities, managers often introduce non-native species when native species can no longer survive in the altered habitat. This aspect was considered in the development of the Public Use section. Goals, objectives and actions for Fisheries Program activities related to Recreational Fishing and Mitigation Fisheries were developed.

Recreational Fishing

Fishing continues to be a favorite pastime in the United States. The Service's 2001 preliminary National Survey of Fishing, Hunting, and Wildlife-Associated Recreation reported that 34 million anglers (16 % of the U.S. population) 16 years old and older, spent more than $35 billion annually on trips, equipment, licenses, and other items to support their fishing activities. The average annual expenditure was $1,046 per angler.

Providing recreational fishing opportunities is a cooperative effort between the Service, other Federal agencies, States, Tribes, NGOs and the sportfishing community. The Service provides various recreational fishing opportunities on lands it manages. At least 268 out of 538 National Wildlife Refuges provided recreational fishing and hosted 6.4 million fishing visits in 2000. The Service also works with the Department of Defense to provide fishing opportunities on military lands.

Recreational Fishing Goal: Quality opportunities for responsible fishing and other related recreational enjoyment of aquatic resources on Service lands, on Tribal and military lands,

and on other waters where the Service has a role. The Fisheries Program will focus its efforts to achieve this goal on the following areas:

Objective 3.1: **Enhance recreational fishing opportunities on Service and Department of Defense lands.** The Fisheries Program will increase its work with National Wildlife Refuges, National Fish Hatcheries, and the Department of Defense to enhance fishing opportunities for the public on Service and military lands. Activities will focus on maintaining and restoring aquatic habitats, developing and implementing fishery management plans, and increasing access for recreational fishing opportunities.

> *Action 3.1.1:* Provide increased expertise and assistance to help develop fish and other aquatic resource conservation elements in Refuge Comprehensive Conservation Plans (CCP's).

> *Action 3.1.2:* Provide increased expertise and assistance to help develop and implement fish and other aquatic resource management plans on National Wildlife Refuges.

> *Action 3.1.3:* Work with the National Wildlife Refuge System to identify and implement ways to increase recreational fishing use on Refuges, where compatible, through actions, such as creating additional access, new habitat, and promotion and outreach.

> *Action 3.1.4:* Advocate for the appropriate involvement of Tribes and State Fish and Wildlife Agencies in activities that involve recreational fisheries, on an ongoing basis.

> *Action 3.1.5:* Provide technical assistance and recommendations for conserving and rehabilitating recreational fisheries on military installations.

Objective 3.2: **Provide support to States, Tribes, and other partners to identify and meet shared or complementary recreational fishing and aquatic education and outreach objectives.** The Fisheries Program will continue to provide hatchery fish and technical assistance in support of recreational fishing and aquatic outreach activities.

> *Action 3.2.1:* Work with States, Tribes, and other partners to provide technical assistance and, under certain conditions, provide hatchery fish to meet recreational fishing objectives (i.e., for mitigation, restoration and recovery of recreationally valuable species, treaty-reserved or statutorily defined Tribal trust natural resources, using conservation exchanges and cost-recovery to optimize fish production, and aquatic outreach and education activities).

> *Action 3.2.2:* Continue to support National Fishing and Boating Week events, scouting jamborees, and similar events with technical assistance and hatchery fish, on an ongoing basis.

Objective 3.3: **Recognize and promote the value and importance of recreational fishery objectives in implementation of other Service responsibilities.** The Fisheries Program will continue its efforts to balance the conservation of native fish and other aquatic resources and providing quality recreational fishing opportunities.

> *Action 3.3.1:* Work with other Service programs to ensure that actions, decisions, policies, and programs consider the recreational fisheries roles and objectives of the Service, on an ongoing basis.

> *Action 3.3.2:* Work with partners to identify and implement outreach and education activities regarding the concept, value, and importance of responsible recreational fishing to the American public.

> *Action 3.3.3:* Conduct a national economic analysis of its contributions to recreational and commercial fishing.

Mitigation Fisheries
When Federal locks and dams were constructed, Congress and the Federal government committed to mitigate impacts on recreational, commercial, and tribal fisheries. Mitigation activities include habitat improvement, native species recovery, and stocking native and non-native fish. Over the years, Congress provided funds and directed the Service to construct and operate hatcheries to provide fish to help mitigate fishery losses. These mitigation hatchery programs are a legitimate use of the National Fish Hatchery System. In some cases, Congress provided funds to others to construct mitigation hatcheries operated by the Service and certain states. Today, the current challenge is to delineate agency mitigation responsibilities and related funding mechanisms.

Mitigation Fisheries Goal: **The Federal government meets its responsibilities to mitigate for the impacts of Federal water projects, including restoring habitat and/or providing fish and associated technical support to compensate for lost fishing opportunities.** The Service will work with other Federal agencies, States, and Tribes to meet mitigation responsibilities, with a focus on the following areas:

Objective 3.4: **Identify the mitigation responsibilities of Federal agencies for Federal water projects.** The Fisheries Program will work with the Administration and Congress to identify and clarify federal agency mitigation responsibilities for federally-funded water projects.

> *Action 3.4.1:* Determine the Service's mitigation responsibilities for federally-funded water projects.

> *Action 3.4.2:* Work with other federal agencies to determine their mitigation responsibility for federally-funded water projects.

Objective 3.5: **Meet the Service's responsibilities for mitigating fisheries at federally-funded water projects.**

> *Action 3.5.1:* Provide fish to meet its determined mitigation responsibilities.

> *Action 3.5.2:* Develop legislative strategies to clarify and authorize mitigation responsibilities for federally-funded water projects.

Objective 3.6: **Recover 100 percent of costs for mitigation activities associated with hatchery production and stocking from the water project sponsor.** The Fisheries Program will identify the full cost of its mitigation activities and increase efforts to pursue cost recovery from the appropriate Federal agencies, involving the Administration and Congress in these efforts. Where full cost recovery is not obtainable, the Service will work with the appropriate entities to identify other means of maintaining the mitigation activities.

> *Action 3.6.1:* Identify the full costs of Service mitigation activities.

> *Action 3.6.2:* Pursue full cost-recovery from other federal agencies for their mitigation responsibilities associated with federally-funded water projects.

4. Cooperation with Native Americans

Conserving this Nation's fish and other aquatic resources cannot be successful without the partnership of Tribes; they manage or influence some of the most important aquatic habitats both on and off reservations. In addition, the Federal government and the Service have distinct and unique obligations toward Tribes based on trust responsibility, treaty provisions, and statutory mandates. The Fisheries Program plays an important role in providing help and support to Tribes as they exercise their sovereignty in the management of their fish and wildlife resources on more than 55 million acres of Federal Indian trust land and in treaty reserved areas.

Native American Assistance Goal: Assistance is provided to Tribes that results in the management, protection, and conservation of their treaty-reserved or statutorily defined trust natural resources which helps Tribes develop their own capabilities. The Fisheries Program will focus its efforts on the following areas:

Objective 4.1: **Provide technical assistance to Tribes.** The Fisheries Program will continue to provide technical assistance to Tribes, as requested and to the extent possible, for Tribal natural resource management activities.

> *Action 4.1.1:* Provide technical assistance to Tribes that supports Tribal natural resource management goals, such as training, developing management plans, maintaining healthy hatchery fish, and developing hatchery operating procedures, on an ongoing basis.

Action 4.1.2: Explore the use of cooperative agreements and Intergovernmental Personnel Act Agreements (IPAs) to advance technical assistance to Tribes and develop Tribal technical expertise in fish and wildlife management.

Objective 4.2: **Identify sources of funds to enhance Tribal resource management.** The Fisheries Program will increase its efforts to work with Tribes and other stakeholders to identify sources of funds that can be used to enhance Tribal resource management infrastructures or for particular partnerships or initiatives involving Tribes.

Action 4.2.1: Work with Tribes to identify potential funds for tribal resource management.

Objective 4.3: **Provide fish for Tribal resource management.** The Fisheries Program will continue to provide fish as part of recovery plans for listed species, in support of sustainable fisheries management, and for trust species and ongoing programs to enhance outdoor recreation on Tribal lands.

Action 4.3.1: Work with Tribes to identify shared or complementary fisheries conservation management objectives.

Action 4.3.2: Provide fish to implement fishery management plans.

Action 4.3.3: Provide fish as agreed to under conservation exchanges or other special arrangements.

Objective 4.4: **Recognize and promote the Service's distinct obligations toward Tribes within the Fisheries Program.** The Fisheries Program will continue to be vigilant that its actions, programs, and other partnerships do not infringe upon tribal rights.

Action 4.4.1: Consult with and integrate Tribes into decisions affecting them to ensure that actions, decisions, and policies consider and integrate tribal roles and responsibilities.

5. Leadership in Science and Technology

Science and technology form the foundation of successful fish and aquatic resource conservation and are used to structure and implement monitoring and evaluation programs that are critical to determine the success of management actions. The Service is committed to following established principles of sound science.

Science and Technology Goal: Science developed and used by Service employees for aquatic resource restoration and management is state-of-the-art, scientifically sound and legally defensible, and technological advances in fisheries science developed by Service employees are available to partners. The Fisheries Program will develop, apply, and disseminate state-of-the-art science and technology to conserve and manage aquatic resources, focusing on the following areas:

Objective 5.1: **Utilize appropriate scientific and technologic tools in formulating and executing fishery management plans and policies.** The Fisheries Program will increase its efforts to identify, revise, and update aquatic science tools as necessary to support the management and conservation of sustainable fisheries.

> *Action 5.1.1:* Work with partners to ensure that all fish and other aquatic resource conservation plans are based on scientifically valid information.

> *Action 5.1.2:* Adhere to the highest scientific standards and ethics in all its activities.

Objective 5.2: **Develop and share applied aquatic scientific and technologic tools with partners.** The Fisheries Program will continue to develop science and technology at its Fish Technology Centers, Fish Health Centers, and Fishery Resources Offices, including its Conservation Genetics Laboratory, and share those capabilities in order to provide a platform for cooperative programs that are beyond the scope of individual States and Tribes.

> *Action 5.2.1:* Work with partners to determine the highest priority needs for scientific, management, and technology tools.

> *Action 5.2.2:* Expand science and technology development to meet priority needs.

> *Action 5.2.3:* Identify, revise, and update aquatic science and technology tools used by the Service and its partners on an ongoing basis.

> *Action 5.2.4:* Increase facilitation for the approval of new and expanded use of aquatic animal chemicals and therapeutic drugs.

> *Action 5.2.5:* The Service Director will work with the Director of the U.S. Geological Survey (USGS) to increase USGS participation in aquatic-related research within the Science Support Partnerships Program and develop more effective mechanisms for Service aquatic resource conservation research needs and priorities to be incorporated into USGS/BRD research activities.

6. Aquatic Habitat Conservation and Management

Loss and alteration of aquatic habitats are principal factors in the decline of native fish and other aquatic resources and the loss of biodiversity. Seventy percent of the Nation's rivers have altered flows, and 50 percent of waterways fail to meet minimum biological criteria.

Aquatic Habitat Goal: **America's streams, lakes, estuaries, and wetlands are functional ecosystems that support self-sustaining communities of fish and other aquatic resources.** The Fisheries Program will collaborate with partners to conserve and restore habitats for fish and other aquatic resource populations, focusing on the following areas:

Objective 6.1: **Facilitate management of aquatic habitats on national and regional scales.** The Fisheries Program will start work with Federal, State, Tribal, and other partners to identify aquatic habitat restoration needs and implement priority actions.

> *Action 6.1.1:* Identify and implement significant watershed management programs with partners to ensure that habitat conservation and restoration is an integral component of management actions.

> *Action 6.1.2:* Work with Federal, State, Tribal, and other partners to explore the benefits of a National Aquatic Habitat Plan and the appropriate Service role in its development and implementation.

Objective 6.2: **Expand the use of Fisheries Program expertise to avoid, minimize or mitigate impacts of habitat alteration on fish and other aquatic species.** The Fisheries Program will increase the involvement of its employees in Service activities to address issues and threats related to hydropower re-licensing and development of wetlands.

> *Action 6.2.1:* Increase Fisheries Program involvement in existing and new Service habitat conservation programs and activities (e.g., HCPs, Partners for Fish and Wildlife, environmental contaminants, FERC relicensing, Refuge planning, and others) to ensure that priority aquatic habitat issues are addressed.

> *Action 6.2.2:* Work with partners to identify and provide access beyond barriers to fish migration.

Objective 6.3: **Increase the quantity and improve the quality of aquatic and riparian habitat on Service lands.** The Fisheries Program will expand the involvement of its employees, in coordination with the National Wildlife Refuge System, to identify and implement opportunities for increasing the quantity and improving the quality of aquatic and riparian habitats on Service lands.

> *Action 6.3.1:* Work with the National Wildlife Refuge System to develop and implement strategies for increased or new aquatic habitat conservation programs on Service lands.

> *Action 6.3.2:* Work with the National Wildlife Refuge System to re-evaluate the Fisheries and Aquatic Resource component of the Land Acquisition Priority System.

Action 6.3.3: Work with the National Wildlife Refuge System to identify opportunities for land protection proposals benefitting fish and other aquatic resources.

7. Workforce Management

The Fisheries Program relies on a broad range of professionals to accomplish its mission: biologists, managers, administrators, clerks, animal caretakers, and maintenance workers. Without their skills and dedication, the Fisheries Program cannot succeed. Employees must be trained, equipped and supported in order to perform their jobs safely, often under demanding environmental conditions, and to keep current with the constantly expanding science of fish and aquatic resource management and conservation.

Workforce Management Goal: Maintain and support an adequately-sized, strategically positioned workforce with state-of-the-art training, equipment, and technologies in their career fields. The Fisheries Program will recruit, support, and position an effective and motivated workforce capable of meeting the expectations of employees and partners in fish and other aquatic resource conservation, focusing on the following areas:

Objective 7.1: **Staff Fisheries Program field stations at levels adequate to effectively meet the Service's goals and objectives in fish and other aquatic resource conservation.** The Fisheries Program will analyze positions and organizational structures at all Fisheries Field Stations, identify the critical staff and functions needed to support various types and sizes of hatcheries and Fishery Resources Offices, and fill critical vacancies or gaps in the workforce with well-qualified individuals.

> *Action 7.1.1:* Develop a 5-year plan to guide human capital management decisions.

> *Action 7.1 2:* Develop and adhere to annual operational work plans for each station.

Objective 7.2: **Provide employees with opportunities to maintain competencies in the expanding knowledge and technologies needed to improve opportunities for professional achievement, advancement and recognition.** The Fisheries Program will identify training and developmental learning opportunities both inside and outside the Service for all skills utilized, as well as preparing staff for future leadership positions.

> *Action 7.2.1:* Identify core competencies required for its employees.

> *Action 7.2.2:* Work with the National Conservation Training Center to develop training opportunities for employees to meet competency levels.

Objective 7.3: **Provide employees with access to facilities and equipment needed to effectively, efficiently and safely perform their jobs.** The Fisheries Program will provide its employees with state-of-the-art biotechnology, computers, and maintenance and safety equipment.

Action 7.3.1: Identify and start implementing operational, structural and geographic changes that would help maximize effectiveness and efficiency at field stations.

Definitions

Aquatic nuisance species - introduced, exotic, or transplanted species, including viruses, bacteria, protozoans, and parasites, that threaten the diversity or abundance of native species or the ecological stability of infested waters, or commercial, agricultural, aquacultural or recreational activities dependent on those waters.

Conservation - management, restoration, and protection of self-sustaining and imperiled species populations.

Exotic species - any species introduced from a foreign country (Shafland and Lewis 1984).

Imperiled species - any species listed as threatened or endangered under the authority of the *Endangered Species Act*, considered a candidate for listing, or its population is in a steep decline.

Interjurisdictional fisheries - freshwater, coastal, or marine fish populations managed by two or more states, nations, or tribal governments because of their geographic distribution or migratory patterns.

Introduced species - any species moved from one place to another by human activity (Shafland and Lewis 1984).

Invasive Species - any non-native species whose introduction does or is likely to cause economic or environmental harm or harm to human health (Executive Order 13112, 1999).

Native species - any species within historic range, the area occupied at the time of European colonization of North America (Horak 1995).

Naturalized species - any non-native species that has adapted and grows or multiplies as if native (Horak 1995).

Non-native species - any species that occupies an ecosystem beyond its historic range (Horak 1995).

Responsible fishing - the act of fishing while 1) abiding to all fishing regulations and laws; 2) preventing the spread of aquatic nuisance species, and; 3) respecting private property and the rights of other anglers.

Self-sustaining - capable of maintaining itself independently (*Webster's New World Dictionary*, Third College Edition, s.v. "self-sustaining").

Transplanted species - any species moved outside of its native range but within a country where it occurs naturally (Shafland and Lewis 1984).

Literature Cited

ASA (American Sportfishing Association). 1996. The Economic Importance of Sport Fishing. 10 pp. American Sportfishing Association. Alexandria, VA.

Dahl, T.E. 1990. Wetland losses in the U.S. 1970's to 1980's. U.S. Department of the Interior, Fish and Wildlife Service, Washington D.C. 21 pp.

Executive Order 13112. 1999. Invasive Species.

Fuller, P.L., L.G. Nico, and J.D. Williams. 1999. Nonindigenous fishes introduced into inland waters of the United States. American Fisheries Society, Special Publication 27, Bethesda, Maryland.

Horak, D. 1995. Native and Non-native Fish Species Used in State Fisheries Management Programs in the United States. American Fisheries Society Symposium 15:61-67.

Miller, A. and B. Payne. 2001. Effects of zebra mussels (*Dreissena polymorpha*) and essential habitat for *Lampsilis higginsi* in the Upper Mississippi River System, 2000. Aquatic Ecology Branch, Engineering Research and Development Center, U.S. Army Corps of Engineers, Vicksburg, MS. 28pp.

Moyle, P.B. and R.A. Leidy. 1992. Loss of biodiversity in aquatic ecosystems: Evidence from fish faunas. In: Fielder, P.L. and S.K. Jans, eds. Conservation Biology: The Theory and Practice of Nature, Conservation Preservation and Management. Chapman and Hall, NY.

OTA, Office of Technology Assessment. 1993. Harmful Non-Indigenous Species in the United States. Washington (DC): Office of Technology Assessment, US Congress.

Shafland, P.L. and W.M. Lewis. 1984. Adapted from: Terminology Associated with Introduced Organisms. Fisheries 9(4):17-18.

Webster's New World Dictionary, Third College Edition. 1988. Simon and Schuster, Inc. New York, New York.

Williams, J.D., M.L. Warren, K.S. Cummings, J.L. Harris, and R.J. Neves. 1993. Conservation status of freshwater mussels of the United States and Canada. Fisheries 18(9):6-22.

Williams, J.E., J.E. Johnson, D.A. Hendrickson, S. Contreras-Balderas, J.D. Williams, M. Navarro-Mendoza, D.E. McAllister, and J.E. Deacon. 1989. Fishes of North America endangered, threatened, or of special concern: 1989. Fisheries 14(6):2-20.

www.ingramcontent.com/pod-product-compliance
Lightning Source LLC
Chambersburg PA
CBHW082205290526
45794CB00008B/3436